The

Leading Lady

Legacy

10 Steps to Becoming the

Leading Lady

of YOUR Life

by Lynita Mitchell-Blackwell, Esq. & CPA
The Leadership Champion

The Leading Lady Legacy:
10 Steps to Becoming the Leading Lady of YOUR Life

Dedication

This book is dedicated to all the women who work daily to make the world a better place and the men who support them.

Acknowledgements

Special thanks to my family for their patience as I developed the concept for this book, and for allowing me time away to bring it to fruition. And thank you to my life coach Alexis Lior and agent Cynthia Walton for their support in bringing the components of the Leading Lady Legacy together.

Heartfelt appreciation to my editor Kathryn V. Stanley for once again making a miracle happen - you are the best!

Preface

The Leading Lady Legacy: 10 Steps to Become the Leading Lady of YOUR Life concept was born during one of my life coaching sessions. I was in the midst of transitioning from the practice of law to speaking and training others full time, and voiced my frustration in finding someone to emulate during the process. (As anyone will tell you, moving from one career path to another is hard. Finding the time to do it as you are running your own law firm is even harder.) My coach listened to my vent, then said to me, "Your path is your own. You decide the *who, what, when, why* and *how*. Let's map out a plan with deadlines to make this happen." And so we did I started by creating a Launch Board, which is a modified vision board with details as to deadlines and action items. During the process, I realized something: we are so focused on being like someone else we forget to be ourselves. How I chose to make the transition will be different from someone else's path because my life is different, my experiences are different, my mind set is different, my temperament is different. You get the point.

A friend of mine once jokingly said to me, "You're not the First Lady. You're the Only Lady!" At the time, I laughed. My husband is, indeed, a pastor, so I am a first lady. Generally, first ladies are placed on a pedestal in religious settings and treated with special care. But you do no need to be married to a minister to be a first lady. You are already the First Lady of YOUR life. As Alexis told me, and now I say to you: "Your path is your own. YOU will decide the *who, what, when, why* and *how*" of everything that happens in your life.

Now I know you are thinking, "Uh, no. I did not decide for a certain thing to happen to me especially that bad one." No, you did not, but you had and still have ultimate control and power over how you deal with it. You are the First and Only Lady in your life. You have that power. And, this book is going to take you through ten steps to help you reclaim and harness that power.

There are no short cuts, instant successes, or any other quick schemes to help you improve your life. Self-improvement is a process that requires dedication and commitment. This process will be even more challenging because I am asking you to focus on YOU-- not your children, husband, or career - just YOU. As women, that is hard because we are constantly caring for and giving to others. But I would ask that as you read this book and work through the exercises at the end, you concentrate on your needs and desires.

My friends, sisters, first ladies, only ladies - let us begin the journey to become our own Leading Ladies!

Part One:
Ten Steps to Becoming Your Leading Lady

1. Find Humor in Everything

2. Live a F.R.E.E. Life

3. Be Courteous and Merciful

4. Wear Your Mink in the Summer

5. Hate the Sin, Love the Sinner

6. Give Yourself A Fresh Start

7. Gather Your "Crew"

8. Clearly Communicate Your Needs

9. Believe in Yourself

10. Engage with Leading Men

Part Two:
Your Leading Lady Revealed

11. YOUR Leading Lady Legacy

12. YOUR Leading Lady Affirmation

13. YOUR Leading Lady Launch Board

Chapter 1: Find Humor In Everything

"There is a thin line that separates laughter and pain,
comedy and tragedy, humor and hurt." Erma
Bombeck

Life is a beautiful process of self discovery, intimate experiences, and rigorous challenges. Our life process shapes the way we view the world and the people in it. We learn how to treat others, and ourselves, based upon these views. The way we treat people becomes rhythmic and has a tempo. Depending on how we "move" in the world, that tempo can be steady, like the beat of a drum, or erratic, like some forms of rock. No matter how you move in this world, your tempo is yours. And once you determine that tempo, you must then determine whether you like it. In other words, **do you like the pace at which you move through life? Are you happy?**

Most people to whom I pose this question stop and stare at me, then look into space for a long moment before responding. I believe the reason that they pause before responding is that most of us have something going on in our lives that keep us from answering with a swift, "Yes". That something may be a child who is having a hard time in school, a supervisor who becomes more critical by the day, or the passing of a friend who you used to talk to every day. I heard a speaker say once, "The storm is always present. Whether you are going into it, in the midst of, or coming out of it; the storm is always present."

In this sense, a "storm" is a challenge or block that is actively and usually negatively affecting your sense of well being. The storm can be big or small, it can be something you directly or indirectly bought about in your life, or it can be something that was set in motion by someone else. No matter the origin or the cause, it is a storm you must get through. And you will get through it in your own time, at your own beat or tempo. And you can do so in a state of happiness or joy. Sounds impossible, does it not? I promise you, this is possible.

One of my favorite movies is *Lee Daniel's The Butler*. My favorite character is the butler's youngest son because he provides much needed comedic relief and levity to the very harsh circumstances underlying this movie. There is a scene when the older brother comes home from an extended absence wearing a black net shirt and leather jacket - attire that was considered unsuitable for the dinner table during that time. During a particularly tense exchange, the younger brother informed his older brother that he would not be able to get into the White House with both nipples exposed - maybe one, but not both. That exchange broke the tension and allowed the family meal to continue (not too much longer, but it did continue). **Sometimes, you have to find the ridiculous in a bad situation to laugh at it and get through it.**

Life requires humor to be bearable. With all the strain and strife in the world, sometimes we have to search hard to find the beauty, but it IS there. And sometimes, we have to make our own beauty out of the ugliness that goes on around us, just like the scene outlined in the movie above. Humor is an easy, painless, and free way to take control of our lives, change the tempo of our grove, and be happy.

Happiness is a state, just as is anger. And like any state, you learn how to move from one to another. One way to do this is with prayer and meditation. I once heard the Honorable Sri Sri Ravi Shankar state that prayer is talking to God and meditation is listening to God's response. What a wonderful way to differentiate the two practices! It takes both talking and listening to God to be happy.

Most of my prayers are filled with one of two things: please and thank you. Please God, help me do the right thing. Thank you, God, for waking me up. Please God, don't let me make a fool of myself. Thank you, God, for my family. Once I am done, I then meditate so I may hear God's response to my petitions.

Meditating is engaging in total silence while seeking peace in the mind. I clear my mind by thinking about dandelions blowing in the wind. During these times I hear God's voice speaking back. I receive inspiration, encouragement, and feelings of peace and love. Sometimes my meditation occurs when I run. The tempo (yes, that again!) of my feet hitting the ground allows me to "zone out" and clears my mind. Many of the points that are included in this book came to me during my morning runs. And when I have a hard decision that needs to be communicated, sometimes the method in which to deliver the news in a kind manner comes to me.

As we move through life and our tempo changes, the way we tap into our inner being and find happiness may need to change, too. I have had the pleasure of taking several courses through the Art of Living Foundation. These courses literally teach how to be happy no matter what is going on in your life. **Through a series of breathing and meditation techniques, learners are trained to refocus our minds and get control of the tempo of our souls.** The organization emphasizes serving others, being a blessing where you are, with what you have.

During my last course with the Foundation, we visited an assisted living facility and delivered groceries to the tenants. The residents were very grateful, which made us feel good, but their circumstances were so desperate that most of us left feeling down because we could not do more. Our facilitators showed us that true happiness is doing the best with what you have. It was better that we took the groceries with the resources that we had then not to have done anything at all. We also became aware of those wonderful seniors' plight and can do more in the future.

We also experienced humor in that very serious situation. I love taking pictures, so I was assigned to be the digital scribe while we were at the facility. I have great shots of our arrival, unloading, and setting up I was tickled by one of the ladies in our group who had to "stop, fix, and profile" for each shot. It did not matter what we were doing, when I turned the camera in her direction, she paused, patted her hair, pressed her lips together to refresh her lipstick and struck a pose. It was so incongruous with what we were doing that I could not help but laugh. I keep the thought of that diva striking a pose in my heart, so I am able to smile when I think about the people in that facility.

I do not pretend to be an expert at being or staying happy. Anyone who truly wants lasting change in her life knows that it is a lifelong process. **I have good days and "cupcakes with wine" days. But I am better than I used to be, and that is huge!**

I also ask people what they do to find humor and stay happy in stressful situations. A couple of my law clients who drove 18 wheelers for a living shared with me an unorthodox but amazingly effective strategy: when someone does something truly ugly on the road, they give them a positive sign. The husband said that when someone curses at him for going too slow, he gives them the "peace" or "thumbs up" sign. The wife said that when something similar happens to her, she blows the person a kiss. I thought that was hilarious, so the next day when a driver who did not see me signal pulled beside me and started cursing me "from here to there" as my granny used to say, I blew a kiss to her. It was amazing! The lady stopped mid rant with mouth hanging open. She seemed to come to herself and realize just how silly she was behaving. That lady turned back to the road, and drove on just as suddenly as she pulled next to me.

In addition to talking with people about what they do to maintain happiness and find humor in situations, I also love to read. I obtained a complimentary copy of *Management Mantras: Keys to Effective Management Leadership* by Sri Sri Ravi Shankar while attending a women's conference in

India. The author encourages people to **smile no matter what, and even if the smile does not begin as true, to "fake it till you make it" (i.e., smile until it is genuine)**. So I tried it one day during a particularly contentious asset division conference where the wife was divorcing the husband because he (husband) refused to work - he had been unemployed three years at that time. We were all sitting at a very small table, and during the course of the proceeding, the husband kicked me in the shin - hard. I jumped and he looked me in the eyes. He said nothing - no excuse me, I'm sorry - just stared at me. I smiled at him. I wanted to kick him back, but I went with my higher thought and smiled at him. He dropped his eyes, and from that point forward, his belligerence receded. When we concluded the conference 45 minutes later, he was the first person to jump up and speed walk to the door, making eye contact with no one.

When I had time to think about the encounter on my way home that evening, the smile I had on my face was from the heart - it was real. And I was able to make a joke about it and laugh with my husband that night. When I told him about it, I ended the story with, "Thank goodness that guy didn't step on my foot, or I might be minus a toe!"

Now there will be times when it is difficult to laugh because you are in so much pain or so stressed out that all you want to do is cry. I have had serious health problems caused by endometriosis (cells that grow outside your uterine wall and attach themselves to organs creating havoc in your body). I have faced money challenges due to downturns in the housing market (I went from closing 80 to 100 loans a month to 7 in one quarter). And I have waded through family crisis (the 2004 death of one of my favorite cousins to senseless violence still sends shutters through my soul). My life tempo changed through each experience, sometimes slowing so that I did not interact with people like I used to; and other times, speeding up so that I was overly involved in social, community and professional activities to block out the pain. The methods I used to be happy and find humor around me changed, too. Movies I previously enjoyed were not so funny to me, so I found new ones to enjoy. Relationships that were previously fulfilling did not feel quite so nurturing, so I developed new ones to nurture me. Tasks that used to relax me became burdens to endure, so I stopped doing them and found other interests.

And you know what? That is alright. It is all right, entirely correct, and the way it should be. You change and grow through life, becoming stronger, more resilient, more peaceful and loving. As you evolve, you are able to become the Leading Lady not just for your life, but for those around you.

So the first step in being the Leading Lady of YOUR Life is to move through life at a tempo that makes YOU feel good, connect with God, and be good to others.

Everyday Women Living the Leading Lady Legacy

Meet Olivia Deneika "Neika" Mitchell. Neika sent a GoFund Me request to a few of her Facebook friends (self included) to raise money for her son's football team. She raised the funds within seven days and 19 days early. Neika sent a message thanking everyone for their contributions, informing us of the campaign's success. And she also asked that we continue giving and encouraged those who had not given already to do so. She explained that this would help other members of the team who were not able to raise the required funds. Neika did not have to send this message, yet she chose to make a plea to her warm circle on behalf of children she has yet to meet and assist parents she may not ever see.

Neika Mitchell is a wife, mother, hair stylist, and everyday woman who lives the Leading Lady Legacy. She moves through life at a tempo that makes her feel good and do good for herself and others.

Chapter 2: Live A F.R.E.E. Life

"I am Finally Released to Experience Expansion.
I am ready to live a FREE life!"
Alexis Lior

When we awake in the morning, we usually engage in the same activity - we hit the ground running! Rarely do we pause to just experience the gratefulness of wakefulness. Our minds awake before our bodies, and it begins to produce a list of things to do before we even open our eyes. Even on days when we do not have to take off like a jet on the runway, we find it difficult to just relax and be at peace in and with the world.

It is important that we take a moment for ourselves in the morning to center and calm our minds. This calmness will set the tone for your day and how you respond to the challenges that arise throughout it. Calmness will mean the difference between stepping out of the bed right onto your child's toy then cursing up a storm versus stepping on that same toy and making a mental note to discuss the importance of putting toys away at the end of the day. Calmness will mean the difference between flipping a bird and spewing curses at a person when he cuts you off when you are running late versus slowing down and allowing that person to pass because the extra five seconds it took is not worth your peace.

My life coach Alexis Lior lives by a very simple code: "**I live FREE**." Alexis' free stands for Finally Released to Experience Expansion. Her social media posts are usually punctuated with #freelife. It is a wonderful reminder that no matter where she is or what she is doing, SHE has ultimate power over how she lives her life. Her inner peace and calmness is just that - it is inner or it is INSIDE of HER. When Alexis and I work through my to-do lists and success logs, we always come back to the same thing: what I want is determined by what I do. If I do not do the work, I will not get the result. It all rises and falls with me, what is inside of me and in my heart. Therefore, it is imperative that I ensure the thoughts and feelings inside me are tempered by peace and calmness.

When my heart is calm and at peace, I am freed to be kinder and more considerate to others. I can really focus on what other people are saying, not just listening "enough" so that I may respond appropriately. I can engage with people, not just verbally, but spiritually as well, discerning their needs without a word spoken. I can be more patient when people are impatient and/or rude with me, giving them a second chance to make a first impression. I can graciously give my time or money for a cause without worrying about how or when I will see a return on this "investment." My girlfriend Mona Shah-Joshi has a saying about this last point, "The universe is keeping better account of karma than you ever could."I am content to allow the Universe its dominion in this area.

Peace and calm are paramount to one's success in life. Yes, there are people in high profile positions with lots of money who are the most ill tempered and unkind creatures you have ever had the misfortune to encounter. But success is more than money and status. It is also joy in life, or as Alexis likes to say living a #freelife. The people you see who are consistently mean to others are not happy. They have not found the tempo of life that makes them happy, that allows them to do good and be good in the world. They are disconnected from the Oneness of All That Is and they are miserable.

To lead a successful, fulfilling life, your tempo must be shared with others. You share your tempo by interacting and engaging with other people. **Being**

genuinely engaged and interested in what others are doing is a good way to do that. This requires more than a few "Likes" on Facebook or following someone on Twitter. True engagement requires picking up the phone and driving by to check on people once in a while. We are all busy, I get that. I am a wife, mother, first lady, lawyer, author, speaker.... (you get the point)... but being busy is not an excuse from disengaging from people in your life. Being disengaged and disconnected leads to a lonely and unfulfilling existence.

One moment of my life where this came into stark relief was Memorial Day Weekend 2013. For the previous two years, I had severe abdominal pain and discomfort that the doctors could not diagnose. By May 2013, I had stopped eating and could only hold down water and PowerAde. I lost 30 pounds in six weeks. My family and friends were worried, but trying to put on a brave front, praying and trusting that I would be healed.

The Friday before Memorial Day, I was admitted to the hospital for emergency surgery. I had a bowel obstruction caused by endometriosis (uterine cells growing outside of my uterus) that was so complicated that they had to remove a piece of my large and small intestines. During my time in the hospital, I had a lot of time to think. I thought about the fact that I had run myself ragged chasing behind people and causes that did not even think enough of me to send a text or email checking on me, but here was my family - some of whom I had not seen or spoken to in months - stacked up in the hospital like sardines all hours of the day, so I would not be alone. I thought about the associates with whom I spent so much time talking with daily to build organizations through the years, but it did not cross my mind to pick up the phone or send a note to let them know I was laid up... it was friends from college and law school who received those messages. I thought about how I had almost missed watching my little daughter become a young woman, seeing her graduate from college, get married, and have her own children because I was pushing so hard to "be successful" that I was not nearly as forceful or aggressive as I should have been in getting a proper diagnosis.

It was this last point that I keep at the forefront of my mind whenever I think about skipping a health-related action for the sake of work. I no longer reschedule my doctor's appointments or skip exercise or eat "mess" for the sake of expediency. **Whatever is going on, it can and will wait.** I am reminded of something my father used to say when my sister and I would worry him about something we wanted and he was taking too long to get it: "Are you going to die if you don't get it now?", he would ask in an exasperated tone. And the answer was always "no." I ask myself that age old question when faced with running late to appointments, missing some "opportunity that will never come again," and meeting some VIP who has the connections and power to "change my life." Am I going to die if this does not come to pass now? The answer is always "no" just it was when I was young

My near death experience also taught me, and allowed me to share with others, a level of forgiveness I had no idea I had in me. One of the first referrals my primary care physician made for me was to a gastro specialist. If that specialist had ordered the proper scans at the beginning of my ordeal, the blockage might have been identified and resolved so much sooner. When I was in the hospital, the gastro specialist came to see me. My beloved younger sister was there and she was so angry on my behalf she could not stand to be in the same room with my doctor. I felt sorry for my doctor. Her shame and guilt were visible on her face. When I was approached about suing her for malpractice, the only thing I could see was that look on her face, and I felt such empathy and compassion for her. In seven years of law practice, I had never been sued for malpractice. I do not know how I would react to being sued for making a mistake, but I can imagine the financial impact would be crippling. In my years of practice, I have never had a claim filed against me or any complaints made regarding my performance, yet my professional liability insurance continues to increase every year, and is now more than half my mortgage.

I was blessed to not only rise from that hospital bed, but to return to active living - a #freelife. In light of my almost full recovery, I could not see punishing my doctor for something for which she was genuinely sorry, and I am almost positive will never happen under her watch again. It was the peace and calm of lying still in that hospital bed that allowed me to see all this so clearly.

Please note that I am not advocating for you to dismiss lapses in your medical treatment, or to allow people to mistreat you in any way. There are too many people who fought and died for all of us to enjoy equal protection under the law. Rather, I am sharing with you my story, my journey, as to how I came to this place in my life. Remember, this is the tempo by which I live in my life. Your tempo will be different.

So the second step in being the leading lady of your life is to take time to be peaceful and calm so you may be successful and live a FREE life.

Meet Vinita Verma. Vinita was the escort assigned to assist my girlfriend Tanika (and by extension - me!) when we traveled to India for a women's conference. Tanika and I were jetlagged beyond reason for the first couple of days. We had a very tight itinerary, but we were late everywhere because we were so tired. Vinita would awake an hour earlier than necessary to escort us where we were supposed to be only to find us still in the bed fast asleep. We would ask for food after the dining area closed (we slept through some of our meals), and Vinita would search high and low to find it, only to return to us food in hand and us fast asleep. I could give you more examples of our unintended flakiness, but I think you get the point. Throughout it all, Vinita maintained her smile. She never allowed OUR sleep deprivation to deprive HER of peace and calm.

Vinita is a mom, business owner, volunteer, and everyday woman who lives the Leading Lady Legacy. She understands that no matter what is going on with other people, she is in total control of her inner peace.

Chapter 3: Be Courteous and Merciful

"When restraint and courtesy are added to strength, the latter becomes irresistible." Mahatma Gandhi

Treating people well is a large part of leading a good life that is worthy of modeling. When we are naturally predisposed to be kind and courteous, we do not have to worry about offending people and causing disharmony. Our minds are focused on creating an environment that is positive and an experience that is joyful. These experiences become memories that may be mentally reviewed, shared, and enjoyed for years to come because we chose to live our best. These are the moments that do not cause us despair or guilt. But...

There are times when we are not treated with courtesy. There are times when our human dignity is insulted. There are times when we go above and beyond to make people feel comfortable and respected, and those same people seem to go out of their way to make us feel the exact opposite. We feel angry, confused, and are ready to retaliate. In those times, be strong and tether your anger. Do not respond rashly or "in kind" to those people. I will not make excuses for them. We have all heard them and made these excuses: the person is just having a bad day, just lost a close family member, is in the midst of divorce, is having problems conceiving, or is unhappy about her weight. The list goes on and on.

Making excuses for people when they behave badly does not help you or them. It puts you in a situation where you enable their behavior, and puts them in a situation where they are not being corrected. Instead of making excuses for unkindness, simply note it and move on. I remember singer and radio host Yolanda Adams once stating that, "Some behavior is not worth acknowledging," when she was complimented on her ability to ignore unkind remarks. Ms. Adams is exactly right - acknowledging unkindness gives credence to the remark, takes away your peace, and pulls you into whatever confusion and drama is going on in that person's life. That is not what you want - you have your own life to live!

In noting the behavior, it is more an internal understanding that the person is behaving badly rather than your call to action to say something to him or her. Remember, the focus here is you. **If you are in a position where pulling the person to the side and having a constructive conversation about the person's behavior will be beneficial, then do so.** But if that is not the case, then keep moving. Do not allow that person's misery to transfer to you. Say a prayer for the person, and keep going.

There are times when we wish we had retaliated against the person for their thoughtlessness or rudeness or downright meanness. In the rare moments when we find ourselves regretting our restraint, remember: it is better to regret what was not said than to regret what was said. People may infer or "think" you were about to say or do anything. But once you have acted on something, there is no taking it back and no time to reconsider. Of course I have been in situations where I had a witty (and biting) "come back" when someone said something ugly to me. And yes, I wanted to wipe that smirk off her face when she made a sly remark to me. But **it takes a much stronger person to refrain from low behavior than it does to say whatever is on your mind.** And it takes a clever person to frame a response in a way that is kind, will be well received, and hopefully taken into consideration, so the person will behave better in the future.

My mother is the Queen of Kind. She and my grandmother were a comedy show. My grandmother was the worst back seat driver ever to grace the interstate. It was so bad that when my generation of cousins obtained our driver's licenses, we would refuse to drive when she was in the car, instead allowing our parents to continue with that privilege. There was never anything you could do that was right. "You're too close that car." "Did you put your blinker on?" "Slow down, there's not enough space in front." This would go on the entire trip. And did I mention my grandmother never had a driver's license and was chauffeured everywhere?

One fine day when my mother had the honor of escorting my grandmother about, she encountered a particularly sharp turn that required leaning far forward to see what was coming from the right. Because my grandmother, in the passenger seat, was leaning forward, too, my mother could not see a thing. In addition to wearing a beautifully high beehive hairstyle, my grandmother had the famous "Williams" head (we have large heads in our family). My mother waited until my grandmother had looked her fill, then said teasingly, "Now that you're finished looking for us, let me take a look, too." My grandmother looked at her, and with a small smile dancing in the corners of her mouth, sat back. That was an incredibly kind way to tell my grandmother to sit back so she could see. How many of us would have said impatiently, "Sit back! I can't see!"? Not too long ago, I would have. But because my mother waited a few seconds and then made a teasing comment, this memory of my grandmother inspires peals of laughter instead of twinges of shame.

You might be thinking it's easier to respond kindly to the small things, but what about the big things? Remember, ladies, it is the small things that roll up and turn into big things. Very rarely does someone blow up over one small thing that is totally unrelated to anything else. Seldom does someone start an argument out of nowhere that is not a continuation of some unresolved skirmish. **Be kind and thoughtful in the "small" things so that they do not become big things.**

Yes, but what about the big things?! Okay, yes I hear you. There will be times when we cannot avoid confronting people about their unmannerly behavior because it is so egregious. In those instances, follow this process: *breathe deeply; choose your words carefully; state the facts; state your feelings regarding the facts; then pause for a response.*

1. Breathe deeply

Breathing deeply helps to cool your core temperature and calm you down. You do not care how it looks, you care how it feels. Take a moment and breathe! This will allow you to expel whatever harsh words were ready to fly from your lips. Breathing is the tether or rope on your sanity. Hold on tightly and do not let go!

2. Choose your words carefully

Taking a moment to choose your words allows you to think through the consequence of saying something you will regret later. Again: don't be concerned about how you look as you take a moment as you gather yourself. Remember it is the person who maintains control who is victorious in these situations. People remember what is said and done, not what is contemplated.

3. State the facts.

Reign in your emotions so that you are able to say exactly what was so offensive. "You said I was fat," is a statement of fact - either the person said these words or they did not. Do not be surprised if the person tries to back pedal and take it back. But move forward with the next step anyway.

4. State your feelings regarding the facts.

By stating your feelings about the facts, you are not getting emotional, rather you are stating your feelings about what was said or done. "I am hurt and embarrassed that you would call me fat, particularly, in front of all these people." Expressing your feelings allows you to air things out so there is no misunderstanding as to what you heard or why you are upset.

5. Allow the person to respond.

Finally, allow the person to respond. But understand, you may not like what you hear. The person may lie or dig in and really "let it all hang out" as my mother would say. Honestly, it is irrelevant to your peace of mind and the calmness of your soul how they respond. The opportunity to respond is a courtesy you are extending to the person who offended you. How many times have you been in a situation where you have tried to respond to someone's accusation and they cut you off or walked away before you can get a word in? Did you not consider that rude? Of course, you did. So in allowing the person to respond to your statement of facts and feelings, you are showing them how to be kind and courteous. You are also giving them an opportunity to apologize.

No matter how that person responds, you are free. You have stated your thoughts and feelings on what has transpired, and are free to create a plan of action about how you will deal with the situation in the future. You may choose to change the nature of the relationship, distancing yourself from the person or severing it all together. You may choose to make a note of the behavior and take it up with a higher authority (in a work situation, for example). You may choose to do nothing at all. But in every instance, you are in control of how you choose to proceed in the future. . You are truly living a #freelife where you are moving to the tempo of your own life, doing good for yourself and others.

So the third step in being the Leading Lady of YOUR life is to maintain control over your person so that you are able to be courteous and kind no matter the situation.

Meet Jennifer Snow. I have known Jennifer since the third grade, and we attended the same schools through high school. We lost touch after graduation, then reconnected via Facebook.

Jennifer has been an incredible supporter of my ventures, particularly the launch of *BOLD Favor Magazine*. She contributed an article in the first issue, and participated in the photo shoot. During the photo shoot, Jennifer's kind brilliance stole the spotlight.

Our makeup artist was running a bit behind schedule. Jennifer needed to get to work, so she did her own makeup, and it was lovely. The problem was that it was not dramatic enough for the camera to pick up, particularly the eyes. I offered to do her eyes, and thought they looked great. Jennifer took a look and said, "Okay, I know you just did this, but I do not like them. I want them to look more like yours." I said okay, and redid them. She inspected her eyes again, and after two more takes, we got them looking grand to her - and the photographer. High five on that!

I am able to laugh and share this story so easily because when Jennifer expressed her displeasure, she was so kind. She did not have an attitude, and her tone was gentle. Her words were straight-forward and based on facts. And we worked together to get her the "look" she wanted.

Jennifer is a daughter, sister, proud aunt, real estate agent, and everyday woman living the Leading Lady Legacy. She understands that kindness and courtesy are imperative to effective communication

that maintains good relationships.

Chapter 4: Wear Your Mink in the Summer

"Take a step back, evaluate what is important, and enjoy life." Teri Garr

Looking good is a large part of feeling good. We tend to tell ourselves that looking good is not the end all of our existence, and it is not, but... The truth is we carry ourselves differently when we know we look great versus when we throw on something just to run to the store. When we like the way we look, we are more likely to feel good about ourselves. Positive energy courses through our veins when we like how we present ourselves to the world. Have you ever watched a small child play dress up? Do you notice that when she places the tiara on her head, shawl around her shoulders, and heels on her feet, she becomes another person all together? Do you notice that she walks with a little sway and holds her hands "just so" as if to say "Look at me, I am important."?

Little darling that she is, that child understands that just by dressing in a way that makes her feel beautiful, she may become whomever she wants to be. Notice that I said "in a way that makes HER feel beautiful."

Looking good in your own eyes is more important than being beautiful to someone else. Society's definition of beauty changes over time. What was stylish in the 1920's was not stylish in the 1950's; what was stylish in the 1970's was not stylish in the 1990's. When you view time through a limitless viewing glass, you see how quickly people's tastes change. **If you rely on others to define your sense of self-worth, you will make yourself crazy trying to keep up with it all.** Focus instead on being beautiful to yourself - however that looks and feels to you.

Why is looking good and feeling beautiful so important? Because how you feel about yourself directly impacts how you view the world and the energy you send to other people. When you are unhappy with yourself, you will look at other people and the things they have with "rose-tinted glasses," believing everything that is "not you" is better: You may think to yourself her hair is thicker than mine, dress fits better than mine, etc. You will start to covet what they have and totally disregard your best qualities. Your longing for "better" sometimes becomes jealousy and envy. Those are powerful emotions that send out negative vibes people can sense a mile away. Smart people will avoid you like the plague; they do not want such negativity in their space, bringing them down.   If smart people leave you in the dust, that leaves the Good Time Bloodsuckers. GTB's feed off negative attention and encourage your discontent to feed their egos. They continue to stoke your feelings of inadequacy until your very life is sucked dry, and you are so involved in their lives that you forget to live and lead your own. This is so not the life you want to live.

You are a beautiful woman. If no one else believes that in this world, YOU need to believe it. You look good. If no one else believes that in this world, YOU must. You are a great person. If no one else believes that in this world, YOU do! And if you need to be a little extra or over the top sometimes to feel good about yourself, then so be it. Life is short, but memories are long. I keep this in mind every time I hesitate to wear something dressy because it may be a little "extra" for the occasion. I ask myself whether I am going to remember the internal battle I am waging, trying to convince myself that the outfit is too much; or whether I am going to remember how pretty I felt as I wore it. The last thought almost always wins, and I wear my necklace that has a bit of "bling," my heels with lace, or my dress with the sash and bow. And each time I go through this mental dance, I think about my grandmother and what she would do - wear it all!

My grandmother was a grand dame. Even at 5'2", she had such regal bearing.   She was a full figured woman with an impressive bosom and curvy figure, and loved wearing two-piece dress suits that accentuated her curves - even in her seventies. As a child, I remember my grandmother coming to a church luncheon one Saturday afternoon wearing one of those fabulous suits, and across her shoulders was a brown stole. One of my mother's cousins saw it, and said incredulously, "Is that a mink?!" My grandmother flipped the tail of that mink over her shoulder and responded as calm as you please, "Yes, it is" and continued to float down the aisle to her seat. My cousin laughed delightedly, as did some of the ladies who overheard the exchange. You see, it was June... in Miami... and my grandmother wore her mink.

It was not until I was in my 30's that I appreciated the nuances of that scenario. My grandmother felt dressed up and classy when she wore that mink. She felt important. She knew she looked good and she felt good when she wore that mink. My grandmother was a beautiful woman with long straight hair to her mid back, but she suffered the scorn that many felt growing up impoverished and as a dark-skinned African American girl in the 1930's. My grandmother was blessed to be raised in a loving family that understood the value and freedom education afforded. By picking strawberries in the summers, and with the help of her siblings, my grandmother was able to save money for her college education. But even after obtaining her degree in Education and obtaining a job as a teacher, my grandmother still experienced colorism, a form of separation due to the color of one's skin. My grandmother had a choice - she could accept the confines of other people's thoughts about who she should be and how much she could have; or she could forge a new way and do her own thing. This mighty woman chose to forge her own way. **She carried herself with dignity, raised her children to do the same, and made sure that if no one else in the world thought she was beautiful, SHE did.** All day, every day.

So at that luncheon years later, my grandmother dressed in a way that made her feel beautiful. She wore her mink without regard to whether or not it was "in season" or fashionable. She did not allow GTB's to bring her down or steal her joy. **My grandmother abided by her own rules and sense of what made her feel good.** She could not have cared less about what anyone else had to say. My grandmother's bearing never changed from the moment she walked into that room, spoke with my cousin, and sat down. She felt fabulous when she left the house, arrived at the church, and during the entire luncheon. It never crossed her mind to allow someone else's sense of propriety change the way she felt about herself or the way she looked.

In that ten-second exchange with my cousin so many years ago, my grandmother taught me more about self-worth and value than many of the books I have read or courses I have attended since. If I could have only remembered that lesson through my teen and young adult years, from how much anxiety could I have saved myself. But the joy is that I remember the lesson now, and can impart that to my daughter.

So now that I am the one who is modeling behavior that will be replicated (children do what they see), I am conscience of the way I govern myself. When someone says something about the way I am attired, the execution of a speech, or how I handled a certain situation, I simply smile and either say, "Thank you" or ignore them, whichever is appropriate at the time. My daughter is starting to pick up some of these habits, and at seven years old, it is working for her. Very rarely do I need to reinforce her view of her own beauty, style, or performance. We are still working on her timing and delivery ("Mommy, why can't I wear my church dress to the playground?"), but that will come with time... I hope.

So the fourth step in being the Leading Lady of YOUR life is to embrace your beauty and

57

sense of style; and value and enjoy life on your own terms.

Everyday Women Living the Leading Lady Legacy

Meet Mona Shah-Joshi. Although born in India, she has lived in the US since she was a small child. Growing up was a challenge, as she had the blended experience of "India" at home and "America" at school. In college, she studied and taught courses in diversity and multiculturalism.

Once a semester, she wore Indian attire to her world lit class. Suddenly, some of her students began perceiving her as foreign or "other." Yet the more Mona continued to learn about India --even

completing an anthropological study on Jain women--
the more she cherished her heritage.

Now as an international wellness speaker and
meditation instructor, Mona travels the world sharing
a message of inclusion and joy in living. And many
times, she does this while wearing her ceremonial
attire, to the delight of her audiences. Mona Shah-
Joshi is a wife, sister, friend and everyday woman
who lives the Leading Lady Legacy. She knows and
values her worth and enjoys life on her own terms.

Chapter 5: Hate the Sin, Love the Sinner

"I am good, but not an angel. I do sin, but I am not the devil." Marilyn Monroe

When I was small, I spent a lot of time with my mother and grandmother. They were both Organization Women, meaning that they were involved with several projects and clubs. They were both natural born leaders, and loved to help and serve others. This required working with different types of people, seeing the good in them, and looking past the bad. When a person performed well, both my mother and grandmother would shower them with generous praise. When a person did not perform to standard, they offered gentle correction and encouraging words. When a person did not perform at all - or "showed out" - my mother and grandmother would shake their heads and move on.

When my mother and grandmother moved on from a person or event, that is exactly what they did - this is not a figure of speech. They would acknowledge that the person was not going to do the right thing or behave appropriately, and move around, over, above, or through them to get the job done. Standing in the way of these iron willed women was a fool's errand, and woe to the person who tried. And several tried over the years. The funny part is that when my mother and grandmother would move on and get things done, they were praised not only by the group at large - but also by the person who got mowed over! It was not until I was in my early 30's that I understood how they did it; and not until my later 30's that I learned the artful skill to do it myself.

Would you like to know their secret? **In the words of Mahatma Gandhi, they learned how to "hate the sin [and] love the sinner."** They literally learned how to separate the person from the act. In doing so, my mother and grandmother were able to address the deed that needed to be done methodically and in a businesslike fashion, yet still care for and respect the person who let them down.

Viewing a person without the tint of their actions is hard because we perceive that their actions are personal to us. We must understand that just as we move through the day consumed with our own thoughts, needs, wants, and desires; so too does everyone else in the world. Their actions reflect their own thoughts, needs, wants and desires. They have very little - if anything - to do with us. So when a person does not come through on a promise, does not perform to standard, or just plain lets you down; more often than not it has nothing to do with you and how they regard you. **They are going through their**

own personal hell and all you can do is pray for them and move on.

A few years ago, I led a women's group where the incoming president seemed to turn from Dr. Jykell to Mr. Hyde over night. She was a good vice-president, but once she got elected, she seemed to fall apart. I received angry calls from people demanding that I intercede. (In hindsight, I should have ignored those calls. I have since learned from that mistake!) I took the new president to lunch and tried to coach her through a few issues. It did not work. Things got worse; people began to behave badly during meetings, projects were not being completed, and the club's reputation began to suffer. I allowed my anger to cloud my view of the situation, so much so that I could not see the president separately from her actions (or lack thereof). I left the group feeling put upon and incredibly disappointed by all that had transpired. In retrospect, I realized that I am more disappointed that I forgot the lesson that my mother and grandmother taught me, one that could have helped diffuse the situation, or at least release a lot of frustration.

If I had "hated the sin, loved the sinner" in this situation, I would have seen that the president was having serious personal problems that were spilling into every other area of her life. I would have seen that she did not want to resign because that would have been an admission of failure that her ego just could not take at that time. And, if the projects and the people the group served were really the focal point of our mission, then a group of us would have banded together to serve those people through some other means.

Years later, when confronted with a similar situation in a different group, I was able to apply what

I had learned and side step the potential fall out entirely. **I put the people - and the entire situation - in a place I call the Bounce House.** The Bounce House is a mental place I have created for people and situations that "act up" and need to be placed in "time out". The Bounce House is my version of loving the sinner yet hating the sin. Bounce Houses are typically used by parents to allow their children to run around and get rid of all that energy. I do the same thing for people or situations that have a lot of negative energy that needs to be expended. Just as parents take children to Monkey Joe's or Chucky Cheese for an hour or two to tucker them out; I, too, place people in the Bounce House. **A person or situation is banished to the Bounce House for a defined period of time to give a chance for all that negative energy** to be released.

How does the Bounce House work? When a person is sent to the Bounce House you ignore phone calls, emails, and avoid any form of communication that would allow the person to disrespect you or a situation bring you down. Sometimes the person becomes angrier, spewing mean-spirited gossip or outright lies. Do not respond. The truth has a way of finding its way to the light, no matter how hard you try to hide it. Trust that the people hearing these untruths will either have sense enough to know there is more to the story and reserve judgment; or they will learn for themselves the error of relying on that person or believing that situation in its current state. This "wait and see" approach works. I have been using it for a few years now with great success.

Once people have exhausted themselves and totally spent their rage, pain, unhappiness, or whatever else has moved them to do things

outside their normal character, you may then allow them to exit the Bounce House. Putting distance between you and other people benefits both parties. It allows you to block negativity from your life, and it allows them to get control of themselves and gain some perspective on their behavior. The Bounce House also helps you avoid saying something you would regret later, making it difficult to reconcile later.

Letting someone burn through their negative emotions is hard, and it is excruciating when you are close. Putting someone you love at arm's length takes strength, discipline, and courage. It also involves risk. There is the possibility that if a person is left out in the cold too long, the relationship will not be as close as it was before or may end altogether. But that is not always a bad thing. Some relationships should be altered because while they are uneven, unfulfilling, or just plain not working for either of you, you were too stubborn or scared to do anything about it. And other relationships should be completely severed because they have run their course - for whatever reason. I have experienced both of these scenarios, and although painful, they were necessary for me to move on with my life and focus on the work that I was called to do without distraction.

I have a girlfriend I have known most of my adult life. From time to time, we place one another in the Bounce House. (Ah, yes, Leading Ladies, sometimes WE are the ones who need a "time out"!) It is hard when we are not in communication, even when it is necessary, because we know one another so well, have been through so much together, and can talk about anything - children, marriage, career, hopes, dreams, and disappointments - everything! But sometimes, she and I have moments where we need a break from one another. We use the Bounce House to preserve our friendship. Sometimes it takes a couple of days to realize when we have been placed in time out because we get caught up in day-to-day life and are busy, but when we do realize it, we talk through the issue so that we can once again be buddies.

One last thing regarding the Bounce House: it is not to be used to exact revenge on a person or cause stress and despair. It is a tool to protect yourself from meanness and negativity, and the other person from totally destroying the relationship you have with harsh words and unconscionable actions.

So, the fifth step in becoming the Leading Lady in YOUR life is to love people, to the best of your ability, but do not allow them to hinder your ability to be happy and live well.

Meet Sonji Willingham. Sonji is a very successful entrepreneur who built a business that became profitable within 18 months, an incredible achievement since most business plans tell you it will take three to five years. During a particularly stressful growth period, Sonji had a partner who did not manage the stress well and began behaving very badly, and the behavior began to affect the business. Sonji had to put that person in the Bounce House: she restricted communication to email, worked from home most of the time, and only responded to critical

matters. It was difficult, but the process worked -
Sonji's former partner burned through the anxiety and
came to self within a few days.

After about a week, Sonji called the person and
had a good, long conversation. Once the air was
clear, they resumed business and went back to work.
Sonji was very clear that the best things she could do
for her former partner was to give the person space
(in the Bounce House) and allow that negative energy
to burn out. If she had not, they may have gotten into
an unnecessary altercation that could have destroyed
their business.

Sonji is a wife, mother, daughter, friend, small
business owner, and everyday woman living the
Leading Lady Legacy. She understands how to give
people the space and time they need so that she may
live happy and well in the life she has chosen.

Chapter 6: Give Yourself A Fresh Start

You may have a fresh start any moment you choose,

for this thing that we call 'failure' is not the falling

down, but the staying down. -- Mary Pickford

Would not life be grand if it we were all

perfect? Imagine a world where we never make a

single error or misjudgment. I think that kind of world

would be pretty awesome, but alas, it is not real. We

all make mistakes. Sometimes we know the moment

it happens: a thoughtless remark, sloppy work,

ignored requests - we hurt people's feelings and we

let people down. That is an unfortunate consequence

of being human; it happens. The problem is not that

we make mistakes, for most of us are mature enough

to admit when we are wrong. The problem stems

from our difficulty in moving on from them.

When we mess up, we get upset. We feel

depressed and sad. And if the mistake is major, we

feel that we will never live it down or get over it. We internalize the emotions so that we get stuck in them, making it hard to move on. We have all seen people who made one mistake and never recovered from it. Mistakes are defining moments. If we are open to them being teachable moments, then mistakes teach us humility, wisdom, grace, and mercy. If we are closed to learning from our mistakes, then we are doomed to make them over and over again.

There is no getting out of or going around mistakes. They have happened, are happening, and will happen all the time. So the best thing is to learn how to learn from them and overcome the negative emotions that come with making mistakes.

When I decided to go out on my own and open my law practice, I was really excited. My husband was excited too and very supportive. We set up my home office, he set up my network (I am all thumbs when it comes to technology), and I got to work cold calling and getting business in the door. I was doing pretty well - only two months in and had already scored my first contract with a sizeable client! I shared my success with a (then) girlfriend who was also an attorney. She was also in a place in her life where she wanted to venture out on her own. We met up to discuss possibly going into a venture together, a partnership. I remembered feeling queasy at the thought because I did not really want a partner; I preferred the autonomy of working alone. But I got scared. I thought about the many drawbacks of working solo: crippling administrative fees of running a successful company, no one being there to cover for me if I got sick, and no one else to bring in business - it would all begin and end with me. So instead of believing in myself and knowing God would provide, I allowed my fear to lead me into a partnership that was doomed from the start and failed within six weeks.

When I realized things were not working out, I did have sense enough to say something. And, although my partner was angry, we were able to part cordially. I apologized to her for not going with my gut. She accepted my apology, but it took me years to shake the feelings of guilt and embarrassment. I berated myself for taking my former partner - and myself - through all those changes. I never knew when it would hit me. I would have a great day in the office, and without warning, I would remember those short weeks we were in business together and my joy would evaporate like water on a hot sidewalk.

I finally got out of that self-defeating place with a simple exercise I practice called "So What If...?" Whenever I find myself in a place where I am mentally beating up on myself or allowing doubts to overtake me, I ask myself, "So what if I had allowed the other thing to happen instead?" And I make myself go through the entire scenario, without rosy embellishments. In applying "So What If...?" to my former partnership, I found that if I had not gone into the joint venture:

> 1) *I would have hurt my girlfriend's feelings and our friendship may not have survived.* In actuality, it did not survive and we are acquaintances now. Although that fear was realized, I survived it.

> 2) *The first time I hit a bump (sickness, lack of client response, etc), I would have thought to myself, "See, this is why I should have a partner, I would have someone to help with this!"* In actuality, the inequity in the workload was a large part of the reason I

wanted to dissolve the practice. This concern never became an issue, and again, I survived.

3) *I would always wonder if I needed another person to drive my success.* **Having someone to help share the load is an incredible blessing, but it has to be the "right somebody."** Just as in a marriage, if two people are to be a powerful combination, they must be equally yoked. My former partner and I were not equally yoked because we had very different ideas as to success and what we wanted out of life. That is not a bad thing it is just the way it is. And this concern was not an issue because I know now after seven years on my own that I can manage success - and failure.

In completing this exercise, I was able to get to a place where I no longer beat up on myself for making this mistake. I will not tell you that I no longer think about my actions and regret them because that is not true. However, I can tell you that the thought no longer makes me want to hide my face in a pillow. It is more like a scar after serious surgery - it is ugly and will always be there, but it no longer hurts when I move.

Let us turn for a moment to how we deal with people who hurt us due to their mistakes. For our own peace of mind, it is important that we handle the situation as gracefully as possible. Why? Because that is what we want from people when we wrong them. Is it hard? Of course it is! But in the words of Tom Hanks in the movie *A League of Their Own*, "It's supposed to be hard. If it wasn't hard, everyone would do it!" We were not built to be strong, soulful individuals for easy work. Let us build our collective grace muscles and put in the hard work.

When people wrong me, I try hard to remember how I felt (and feel) when I have hurt someone else or let them down. Sometimes it is difficult to be so compassionate, especially when I am still suffering the effects of their behavior - and more so when the action they took was deliberate. **But forgiveness has a healing power for both the person giving it and the person receiving it.** It allows both persons a fresh start, a way to move on with life. The moving on part of life is how we build our grace muscles. We have to push ourselves past the feelings of pain and betrayal, and continue to move forward as fast as our minds and hearts will allow. As we continue to move, we get better at moving on, so that it gets easier with time. Just as it gets easier to work with hand weights as we practice repetitions during our workouts, so too does it get easier to move on when we are wronged. But like any effective workout, it takes effort to get results. In other words, forgiving people still requires work - you will sweat, you will exert yourself, you will be uncomfortable, you will want to quit, but if you stick with it, you will get the results you desire: strong grace muscles to push toward a fresh start!

True forgiveness is not forgetting and it is not immediate. True forgiveness is a process, and just like a workout, some days it is easier to endure that process than others. Think about it: have you ever been offended to the point of tears (or rage) and some days when you think about the situation you feel fine, and other days the thought of what happened is as fresh today as it was the moment it happened? On the good days, thank God for allowing you to be free of the pain. And on bad days, ask God to give you strength to keep moving toward another good day. Eventually, you will have more good days than bad, and that painful memory will become but a scar in your life experience. An unattractive remembrance? Yes but one that does not stop you from moving forward in life.

So step six in becoming the Leading Lady in YOUR life is to accept that there will be missteps in life; forgiveness and grace are the only thing holding you back from a new beginning - for yourself and others.

Everyday Women Living the Leading Lady Legacy

Meet Sonja N. Brown. Sonja is the prayer leader of a group called Designed for Destiny. Every Wednesday morning, she leads a group of women through a powerful half hour of prayer and inspiration. One of the reasons our sessions are so awesome is that Sonja uses real world examples to drive home her points so that things are practical, not just theoretical. During one of these examples some time ago, she was overly critical of a person who did something she did not agree with. After the session, one of our group members contacted her and told her that she was overly critical regarding that situation. Incredible woman that she is, Sonja posted a message to social media apologizing for being harsh and thanked the person who called her.

In not making excuses and apologizing immediately, Sonja was able to move on from this misstep, and has continued to conduct powerful sessions of inspiration and empowerment that reenergize our group until the next time.

Sonja is an attorney, minister, daughter, sister, and aunt who understands that in owning her misstep and forgiving herself for it, she was able to make her

own fresh start.

Chapter 7: Gather Your Crew

"My friends and family are my support system. They tell me what I need to hear, not what I want to hear and they are there for me in the good and bad times. Without them I have no idea where I would be and I know that their love for me is what's keeping my head above the water." -- Kelly Clarkson

The importance of having a strong support system cannot be overstated. To be successful in any endeavor, you must have friends and/or family who are *for* you 100%. There is no such thing as pulling yourself up by your own boot straps - somewhere along the line, someone showed you kindness, mercy, and helped you - whether you knew it or not. People who do not comprehend their need for a support system are sad, confused human beings who do not understand the interconnectivity of All That Is, nor do they understand the power and joy of relationships and community. It is the people we love who make life worth living and success worth having.

I have been very blessed to experience success throughout my life. But I understand that none of it would be possible without the Five Two and Under Crew (5'2" & UC). My husband is an honorary member since he is male and 6'1"; but most of my Crew are small women. I laughingly tell people, "Find little women - they work hard!" My mother and agent both fit this bill as do two of my mentors. Now, of course, every person who has helped me along the way does not fit the physical specifications of 5'2" & UC, but they meet every other qualification.

I know your brow is furrowed wondering what I mean by qualifications. Yes, I have standards about who I consider to be part of my inner circle. I have colleagues and acquaintances; and then I have friends and family - THOSE are the people in my

Crew. So I'm sure you're wondering what my standards are.

1) **Committed. My Crew has my best interest at heart, and wants me to do well.** They understand that I feel the same way about each of them and will work my heart out to ensure all that is good comes their way. My Crew goes above and beyond the call of duty, and knows that I will do the same. When I need something, I can call and we will work out how it is going to happen - together - and they know that I will do the same, even if it is my last $10. If I eat, they eat; when I prosper, so do they. **We rise and fall together.**

2) **Connection.** I am in contact with my Crew. This is beyond social media. **We talk on the phone, via email, via text - we communicate.** We do not talk every day, but I know what is going on with them - and they with me. When I was in the hospital, my

Crew knew and saw about me. Some were not able to physically come to my bedside, but they checked on me (and blew up my sister's phone to get updates). My Crew knows that if I find out that they are in a bad way and they do not tell me, we are going to have serious words - after we work through the situation.

3) **Honest. My Crew tells me the truth, no matter the consequences.** I may not like their assessment of a situation, but I know what they say is from the heart and is being put forth to help me succeed, not to bring me down. My Crew knows that if I offer criticism, something must be pretty bad; my tolerance for "out there" is high, so if I am saying something, the situation needs to be corrected pronto. When being honest, we do not always agree, but we disagree respectfully.

4) Understands Me & Where I'm Trying to Go. - **My Crew knows, understands and supports my hopes and dreams.** They work almost as hard as I do to make them happen. Sometimes they are working while I am moping and feeling down. And when they are down, I get to work pumping them up and helping to get things back on track until they are "right" again. My Crew wants me to achieve all I put my mind to - not only those dreams that are reasonable, but the wild and crazy ones, too. They understand that if they help me reach those "out there" goals, they will always be able to take credit for making it happen. In turn, I love being part of my Crew's crazy schemes. How much fun we have putting our minds together to make things happen!

Your Crew takes years to establish and develop; and a lifetime to maintain. **There are core members and supporting members.** Core members of your Crew rarely change. Some of us are blessed that those core members consist of our parents, siblings, aunts, uncles, cousins, and grade school friends. Others have to build their core Crew from scratch - co-workers, organizational colleagues, and relationships developed while trying new things. My Core Crew is a mixture of both. **It does not matter whether a person is bound to you by blood, marriage, or friendship, as long as the rope is made of love.** They need only love you and all that you aspire to become.

Your Supporting Crew members are those who come into your life for a defined period of time and for a defined purpose. Once that time or season has passed, the purpose fulfilled, they move on. While these persons are loyal, connected, honest, and understand you and where you are trying to go; their own priorities compete with yours, and once your goals are no longer complement theirs, the Supporting Crew naturally falls away. Supporting Crew members are necessary for our growth and development. We need new people in our lives to challenge us, give us new information, show us different (and sometimes better) ways of doing things, introduce us to new opportunities, bless us with new experiences that give us courage and experience, and generally help move us along so we do not become stagnant. We help our Supporting Crew members do the same: they learn from and are challenged, inspired and blessed by our presence in their lives.

Sometimes we know when a person is a Supporting Crew member, and although letting them go is not easy because we still love and care for the person, the end of your journey together comes to a natural conclusion and is easy to accept. Other times, we are caught off guard when the transition occurs because we thought the person was part of the Core. When the person transitions out of our Crew, we feel a void and it hurts. Do not allow that pain to keep you from connecting with other people. Pain is part of living; it will pass. Open yourself to the joy of meeting new people who can and will lift you to unexpected adventures and joy.

One of the most beautiful interactions of Crew members being there and doing what needs to be done is that of a mother being a Core Crew member for her child. Watching people push past discomfort and fear for the sake of their child is a powerful inspiration. The mother of one of the children my daughter plays with is an example of such a person. Her six year old son is so prim and proper being around him is like being in the presence of a US President. Whenever I see the little darling, I am compelled to sit up straight in my chair and smooth my dress. He is always so sweet and gentlemanly to my daughter and I just love him. I was excited to finally meet his mother, so I could tell her what a wonderful job she was doing raising him.

Little POTUS' mother was not what I expected. Her black hair was long with fire red highlights, her eyelashes were the length of a third of my pinkie finger, and she had an incredibly colorful tattoo that wrapped around her neck, down her shoulder, and into her dress which was, by the way, fitted and short. But it was her eyes that got me. Her large brown eyes were determined, yet cautious and guarded. While most everything about her seemed foreign to me, as a mother, I understood the look in her eyes. She was determined her child would get every opportunity that every other child had, and she was guarded because she knew she did not look like the other parents, and was not sure how we would react.

Most of the parents present that day work in an office and were dressed in office attire. But I promise you, if she had been dressed as Elvira, I would have behaved the same way. I shook her hand and told her how much I appreciated her incredible son and his attention to my daughter. I complimented her on his beautiful manners and stately bearing. She smiled hesitantly, then fully once she realized I meant it. I introduced her to my husband, and once she saw that he shared my gratitude, little POTUS' mom visibly relaxed. She thanked me and we chatted like old friends.

I respect the courage it took that wonderful woman to come into that room with all of us. It is hard when you do not know anyone in a room, and harder still when you do not look like everyone else there.

But little POTUS' mom was not going to allow her own discomfort to cause her to miss a key part of an orientation that would help her son. She is the pillar Core member of her son's Crew.

Just as you can be a part of your children's crew, they can be a part of your crew too. My seven year old daughter is a part of my Core Crew. As small as she is, she gets that mommy is trying to do big things and from the time she could walk she has been there helping to make things happen. I did not understand just how in tune she was to me and my projects until one day after we launched *BOLD Favor Magazine*. My daughter said to me, "Mommy, *we* have a new fan of *BOLD Magazine*!"   I am amazed at the fact that she had said *we* not *you*. It said to me that she owned and supported my dreams and goals. With tears in my eyes, I replied to her, "Yes baby, *we* do." A few weeks later when she introduced herself to a new girl on the playground she said, "Yes, my mom and I just launched *BOLD Magazine*. It's really good." I almost fell over in shock, but I should not have been surprised. Even at her young age, my child meets all the standards I set forth to be part of my Crew. When it comes to who is your Crew, age is nothing but a number.

The seventh step in becoming the Leading Lady in YOUR life is to identify the members of your Crew, and take care of them with the same love and loyalty you expect from them.

Meet Sharon Martinez. I have known Sharon since high school. She was a bride's maid in my wedding, the first person to purchase her plane ticket for our 15 year vow renewal celebration, and the first person to purchase my first book *Leading Through Living: A Guide for Women Seeking Growth Through Leadership*. She promoted that book as if it were her own, posting on Facebook and encouraging friends and family members to buy it. When I launched *BOLD Favor Magazine*, she did the same thing, and hooked me up with an awesome photographer to feature in the next edition.

Sharon is a member of my Core Crew. She is fiercely loyal, we stay connected no matter what, we are honest in all things, and my dreams are her dreams and vice versa. Sharon is a teacher, daughter, sister, lover of cats and loves the members of her Crew with the same love she has for herself.

Chapter 8: Clearly Communicate Your Needs

"In finding love, I think it's important to be patient. In being in a relationship, I think it's important to be honest, to communicate, to respect and trust, and to strive to give more than you take." -- Kina Grannis

What do you want out of life? If someone asked you that question - right now - could you answer it? How long would it take you to do so? It is a tough question that most of us do not dare analyze. Why? Because it would mean that we have an obligation to take action. It is imperative that we answer the question "What do I want?" because if we cannot articulate it to ourselves, how do we expect to communicate it to other people?

Understanding what makes you happy and drives your spirit is a process. It requires you to be patient with yourself as you review your life and things that have made your heart sing. It requires honesty as you face the things that make your stomach lurch. It also requires courage to acknowledge the decisions you made to lead you to this point in your life. This is a wonderful place of self-reflection and discovery that will help you to understand why you did what you did, and how to do things differently to get the results you desire.

When we use the term *communicate* it is usually in relation to other people. But we must first learn how to effectively communicate with ourselves. Sometimes we are so focused on getting along and gaining approval from others that we convince ourselves that things that we cannot stand are actually ok, or even better than ok- that they are grand! You do not believe me? I know a woman who was married to a man for over 20 years and knew him to be gay from the moment they met. She wanted to be married. They got along well, and had such similar goals and aspirations that she convinced herself that sexual intimacy was not important. For years, she ignored her physical needs and convinced herself that she was happy. Outwardly, their lives were perfect: beautiful children, great careers, fabulous home, and active social life. It was not until the children were grown and gone that she admitted to herself that she found the union unfulfilling on many levels and asked for a divorce.

For the sake of convenience and to mitigate her loneliness, this woman convinced herself that physical intimacy was not important and confined herself to a marriage that left her unfulfilled. It took her over 20 years to say that to herself, and a bit longer to say it to her husband and the world. (She shared this story in a public meeting.)

Telling someone what you want and need takes courage. People, in general, and we as women specifically, are so concerned about hurting someone else's feelings that we suffer in silence, pushing our own desires to the bottom of the list of priorities until we almost forget what was on the list in the first place. But notice I said "almost." We never really forget our hopes, dreams, and burning desires of our heart. Eventually those things rise up and become so tantalizing that we can no longer deny them.

It is in that moment that breakthrough comes. You know that there is something you want, something your very soul needs, and you are now in a place that you can deny it no longer. This is a good place, a great place! It means you are ready to take action and work on your happiness. Part of that work is communicating what you want to others. Often times, communicating what we want to others is where fear comes in, and threatens to put the brakes on your entire process. You wonder:

-How am I going to tell my husband that I have changed my mind about my career?

-Will my adult children understand and be supportive when I tell them I want to remarry?

-What are my friends going to think when I tell them I want to move half way around the world and start a new adventure now that I am retired?

These questions whirl in your mind, tearing through your peace like a tornado through a small town. You feel out of control and paralyzed with fear. But you are in control. Each of the above questions is framed with power because YOU are the one doing the telling. . Each question embodies "I am going to tell." I, me, my - this is your way of asserting your power. YOU are communicating to your loved ones your goals and desires. You are not hoping they will get the hint and guess. You are not waiting for them to come to it on their own. You are not allowing your life to pass you by as you hope for permission from those you love to do the thing that makes you happy. You are telling them what you need to feel good about your life. You may not be sure of the exact words - yet - but the telling is going down anyway.

Let us talk a moment about finding the right words and the right time. When it comes to communicating important news, there is never a "right" time. The best time to do it is when you have the courage. There will always be someone who disagrees with the way you deliver the news, where you deliver the news, that you delivered the news at all - so you may as well just get it over with.

The right words are those that communicate your desires in a courteous manner. There actually is a kind way to ask for a divorce. There is a kind way to state you are resigning from your job. There is a kind way to ask a long term house guest to leave. Use the same process you used when expressing your distaste of unmannerly behavior: **breathe deeply; choose your words carefully; state the facts; state your feelings regarding the facts; then pause for a response.**

And just as before, you may not like what is said in response. Your spouse may not want a divorce. Your children may not want you to find solace in the arms of a man who is not their father. Your friends may not be happy you are enjoying your retirement traveling around the world. So be it. You have said what needs to be said and are ready to move on with what makes you happy.

It is imperative that you are set on what you want before you communicate it to others. Communicating exactly what you need sometimes opens the door to negotiation. People do not like change. They will try to make deals to keep things just the way they are even if they are not content with the situation. For some the devil they know is better than the one they do not know. Stand strong and go forward with what you had in mind. Trust and believe –that you have made the right decision for this time in your life.

I had the pleasure of working as an executive recruiter before I opened my law firm. Our firm was small, so we always knew who was working on what. And inevitably, someone would have a candidate who came in so sure that they wanted to leave their job, we would work hard to get an offer for them, they would hand in their notice, only to have them decide to stay at the old job. We would talk until we were blue in the face, trying to convince them that this was a bad move. No matter what we said, they had a counter to it, and would have US turn down the other offer. Without fail, within six months of this fiasco, that same candidate would return, hat in hand, begging us to help them get out of the position they had returned to because conditions had become intolerable: their employer was treating them worse than before; they made more money, but had more responsibility; they did not enjoy the same flexibility with schedule as they did before; and so on. But how and why does this happen?

When you communicate to someone that you are not happy in a situation but do not give them an opportunity to rectify it, you must be prepared to move on. When you deliver the news, the other party is blindsided so they react with their gut. Their gut feeling is usually to keep things status quo. So they pull on your emotions, invoking past good times all in an effort to change your mind. You feel nostalgic for the old days or guilty for leaving them in a lurch or fearful of change-- and decide to forego your plans. But here is where things get tricky: now the other party knows that you are unhappy. Once the shock wears off, they begin to look at you a bit differently, and their behavior starts to change. Things do not ever go back to exactly what they were before. Sometimes things improve, even if it is only for a short time. But other times, they get worse. And you wind up in a position where you must communicate the same frustration to the other party.

Now this is not to say that people do not deserve second chances, that decisions should not be reconsidered when new information is introduced, nor that you cannot change your mind. Changing your mind is always on the table. After all, it is your life. Rather, it is to say that before you allow your emotions to get the better of you and you start popping off about how a particular situation makes you unhappy, you should take time to consider what will actually make you happy. Then you may communicate that in a courteous manner to the parties involved.

One final point about communication your desires. Communicating a desire to change circumstances should not be used as a power play to manipulate someone else's behavior. Choose to communicate things that are truthful, honest, and loving. Do not use communication as a way to manipulate, use it to speak your truth in an honest and loving manner. This book is about living a good life filled with self-love, empowerment, and championship leadership. These ideals are served when you focus on you and being the best person you can be, not trying to coerce someone else into being the person you want them to be.

The eighth step in becoming the Leading Lady of YOUR life is to understand your wants

and needs, and communicate them in a courteous manner once you are comfortable and sure of your action.

Meet Jewel Anderson. Jewel is an incredibly supportive friend and advocate. She agreed to serve as campaign manager for an acquaintance and at first it was great. Jewel learned a lot of new things, met a lot of people, and guided the candidate through a very contentious race. However, during that experience, Jewel realized that she was using the campaign to hide from her own vision and calling. In light of this revelation, the stress, other responsibilities and aspirations, Jewel knew that she would not be able to continue with the campaign should a run off result. Jewel stayed through the primary, and made the decision that it was time to leave. It was the hardest decision she had made as a leader up to that point, but knew it was necessary. Jewel communicated this professionally to the candidate, and they mutually agreed to the separation.

Jewel is a career coach, magazine founder, daughter, friend, and everyday woman living the Leading Lady Legacy. She knows that understanding her needs and communicating them to others in a respectful manner are paramount in being happy and joyful.

Chapter 9: Believe in Yourself

"Some people say I have attitude - maybe I do... but I think you have to. You have to believe in yourself when no one else does - that makes you a winner right there." --Venus Williams

Why is it easier to believe in someone else, but so hard to believe in ourselves? Why is it so easy to believe that someone else is going to complete some big project or has the requisite knowledge for some big task or know the people necessary to get some big hook up while not believing we have the knowledge and abilities? Why do we believe that other people's ability to present themselves in a glowing light automatically relegates our own brilliance to little more than a dull glow?

I believe I have the answer to these questions. **It is easy to believe in someone else with greater intensity and passion than we do ourselves**

because we do not want the responsibility that comes with knowing how brilliant we actually are. Once we realize what great speakers we are, there is now a responsibility to speak up in the face of injustice. When we realize what great writers we are, there is a responsibility to write Op-Ed pieces that challenge the status quo. When we realize how good we are, we realize that there is a responsibility to teach others to be better. I believe that we sell ourselves short simply because we do not want any more responsibilities crowding our already stressed and burdened lives.

We are presented with a classic *Catch 22* situation. We do not want the responsibility that comes with the knowledge of our greatness, but we also do not want the distress and depression that comes with feeling inadequate. God bless us, we do not know what we want! This confusion as to what we want and why comes from not living our lives as our own Leading Lady. **Once we acknowledge all that we do well, and commit to sharing that with the world, we can drop the pretense of living for others' approval because truth be told those whose approval we seek are also seeking others' approval.** This may sound convoluted and confusing, so let me give you an example that I hope will make this concept crystal clear.

When I had my own law firm, I primarily focused on secondary transactions in residential real estate, i.e., I completed refinances, home equity loans, lines of credit, modifications, assumptions and reverse mortgages. I had intimate knowledge of the clients' personal and financial lives; oftentimes more so than their spouses. Sometimes I would have the pleasure of seeing the properties and homes that secured these transactions. I would wonder how in the world someone who made about what I made could afford a $1,000,000 home with a new Mercedes and golf club membership. Sometimes I would feel unsure of myself and wonder if I should be the one handling their transaction, wondering if someone with more experience and education and better connections and better this or that should be handling the transaction. Though I would wear a mask to hide my discomfort, it was still there undermining my self-confidence.

But then I started paying attention to the financials, and things changed forever. These poor people, who I had thought were doing so well and living so grandly, were in debt up to their eyeballs. They had second mortgages, lines of credit, and several credit cards that were charged in the tens and sometimes hundreds of thousands. Although they had high paying jobs, every dime was accounted for and then some. That is when I understood that the pinched look around their eyes was not just from a long day, but from a long spiral of despair. They could not see how to get out of this pit.

These poor people were living above and beyond their means to keep up with the Joneses. The Joneses are people who we admire and if given the chance, would take over their lives today without hesitation. The Joneses are perfect. They have the house, car, spouse, kids, and careers we envy. They take incredible vacations, have the latest gadgets, are members of the best clubs, and enjoy only the finest cuisine at the best restaurants. The truth is the Joneses do not exist. They are a myth! I know this because sometimes the very people my clients were trying to emulate and impress were in the same debt-hell predicament because they were trying to emulate and impress another set of Joneses!

Once I realized just how miserable the people I thought "had it all" were, all feelings of inadequacy and uncertainty left my soul. Instead, I felt compassion for them and would pray for them once I left their presence. I even prayed for the ones who worked so hard to make me feel as if I were nothing more than a servant doing their bidding as opposed to a professional who was there to help them conduct business. (In spite of all my degrees and certifications, I still encounter people who strive to show me just how base and discourteous they can be. In the words of the late Dr. Maya Angelou, "And, still I rise.")

As a result of this experience, I learned some critical lessons in being the Leading Lady of MY life. **The first was that I had to like myself.** I had to like myself, what I was doing, and how I was doing it. I needed to respect my work ethic, the way I conducted myself, my "polish" and acumen. If there were things I needed to change for ME then I did it. More importantly, drawing comparisons to my version of the Joneses ended.

Once I liked myself, I learned to love myself. I learned to love the way I felt when I had done a good job, loved the way I made people feel when we parted, loved the fact that I was helping to make the world better one lowered interest rate or monthly payment at a time.

And once I loved myself, I could and did believe in myself. I was able to battle back with vigor when challenged (politely, but still with vigor). I was able to try new things and be happy when they worked out, and laughed when they did not. I was able to calmly smile and remain unruffled when a client insinuated that I was stupid because she did not understand her own financial situation.

When you believe in yourself, you develop a certain swagger or "swag." You radiate power and people say "You have great presence" before you've even said a word. You look at yourself, with all the lines in your forehead, wrinkles around your eyes, and cellulite on your bottom, and can say, "Hey there, pretty lady! We are going to take over the world today!" People sense how great you feel about yourself, and they start feeling that way about you, too. Pretty soon, other people start believing in you, rooting for you, believing that you can do all the things they cannot. You may have to start telling them, "I slept at a Holiday Inn last night" to explain your greatness! (Just kidding.)

And now that you have this swagger, and the hopes and dreams of others on your small shoulders, you have an obligation and duty to do something good with it. Now is the time to focus on making your life and the lives of those around you better. This is not a charge to run for President of the United States (although if you did, I would be right there behind you screaming, "Go sister go!"). Rather, this is a bold charge to work to make the world better one act at a time. Remember, you have total control over you, so start there to turn distressed into de-stressed. Do what you can with what you have. You can teach someone a new skill. You can share a joke to make someone who is sad smile. You can donate time or resources to a cause you support.

The ninth step in becoming the Leading Lady of YOUR life is to like, love and believe in yourself.

Meet Pamella Wallace. Pamella became a mother for the first time at 17. She completed high school and had two more children before she was 20. Life was very hard. Although she had some family support, it was not as strong as it could have been. Some of her friends - and a few family members - were very negative, convinced that neither she nor her beautiful daughters - Mercedes, Felicia, and Jasmine - would amount to much. Pamella did not allow their snobbery and meanness to stop her from providing the best home and education she could. She worked her way up to manager at a popular food chain, putting in long, hard hours. Her daughters saw how hard Pamella worked, and they rallied around their mother, digging into their studies and extracurricular activities during the year and working during the summers. All of Pamella's children received scholarships to attend college and are enrolled full time.

Pamella Wallace is a mother, sister, manager, and everyday woman who lives the Leading Lady Legacy. She understood that if she and her girls were going to make it in this world, she had to like, love, and believe in herself.

Chapter 10: Engage with Leading Men

"No [wo]man is an island." -- John Donne

Life is meant to be enjoyed with others. While I enjoy my solitude, I also enjoy the company of family and friends. I enjoy times spent with my sisters, basking in their strength, warmth, and love, but I also need time with my brothers. **Every Leading Lady needs a Leading Man.**

A Leading Man is not necessarily a lover. My first Leading Man was my father. My favorite picture of all time is one where I am about one and he 41, sitting on the side of a pool with our matching bellies hanging over our swim suit bottoms. My dad taught me the importance of fair dealing and honor in business as well as friendship. He taught me that love is unconditional, encompasses unlimited forgiveness, and will always be shared between us. My dad was the first man to tell me I was beautiful.

I am blessed to have a husband who has the same positive qualities as my father. I enjoy watching him impart these valuable lessons to our daughter, and look forward to the day when she will find a man - consciously or unconsciously - like her dad to do the same for her children. But I am aware that she may not marry at all, as evidenced by several of my friends and family members who have remained single. If that is the case, I would like to know that she knows what to look for in a Leading Man, a person who will support and nurture her - a man (or men) who are worthy to be part of her Crew.

There are other men outside of my father and husband who I consider to be Leading Men because they embody all that I love and respect about men. They have what I call CHROME: Charisma, Honor, Resourcefulness, Optimism, Manliness (swagger), and Excellence. I admire these gentlemen of CHROME. They are men like

- Andrew Mariner who taught me the art of sales from the ground up.   Andrew took me under his wing, teaching me how to cultivate relationships and working deals with me from start to finish. He was genuinely happy for me when I won business and proud of my success, and that continues to today. All these years later, when I call him to catch up and check on him and his family, he answers the phone, "Is this Rock Star Lynita?"

- James Reid, who lives thousands of miles away, yet supports everything I do including writing for my magazine, helping with online formatting issues, and sharing on social media - all for free because he is my friend.

- Mario Cobian who founded and largely funds LiT College Tour, a non-profit that travels across the country to bring together business leaders and entrepreneurs to train and mentor minority and disadvantaged youth to be leaders.

CHROME men are committed to supporting people and helping them accomplish great things. They are not perfect, but we do not need them to be perfect people. We need them to be Leading Men.

Surrounding yourself with CHROME men is not just a luxury, it is a necessity. **Female friendship is beautiful, but so is male friendship.** Emphasis is on the word friendship. One of my favorite movies is *Pacific Rim*. Yes, it is an action movie involving aliens and gigantic robots, but stay with me for a moment. The robots that defend the earth from the aliens are powered by two individuals who must be "drift compatible." Drift compatibility requires a closeness and connection between the two people so that the robot functions to its full capacity. This level of intimacy has nothing to do with sex. The two main characters - a man and woman - who were found to be drift compatible, although incredibly close, never had sex nor kissed once in the entire movie.

Finding CHROME men with whom you are "drift compatible" can really expand your horizons. Men generally have a different perspective from women on various things - sometimes that perspective is useful, other times it is comical. Either way, your time is not wasted hearing from someone outside of your female warm circle.

CHROME men have a way of cheering you up when you are down that is uniquely male. When I have had a particularly frustrating day, my husband does not ask me if I want to talk about it like a girlfriend would; he holds me until I fall asleep. And if I am talking with my friend Dale about some bone-head thing a client said, he will respond with something along the lines of, "So? Did you get paid? Well then!" Well, indeed.

CHROME men are usually willing to serve as your mentors, helping to guide you through career situations that may involve subtleties that you miss. Of course your female friends can do the same, but remember, we are talking about expanding your circle and taking full advantage of a different set of eyes on the task at hand.

Leading Men teach you what to look for in a companion. Because of the love and respect my father had for me as a young woman, I knew I would settle for no less from my future husband. For my sisters whose fathers who were not present in your lives, your male relatives and friends can and will give you the support and insight you need in selecting a suitable mate. Even if they do not treat women like queens, your male associates can teach you the tricks and pitfalls to avoid, and what you should not tolerate in a relationship. Knowing what to avoid is just as important as knowing what to look for in a companion.

Leading Men also teach other men how to treat you. When my mother was sick, she asked one of my cousins to go to the bank to get some money out of the ATM. He withdrew the amount, and then did a second transaction to get more money. My mother found out what he did when a couple of her checks were returned unpaid. When she confronted my cousin about it, he made excuses, but did not move to return the funds. I was upset and told my husband about it just to vent. My husband was furious and made it clear to my cousin that he was not welcome in our home until he made things right with my mother by repaying the money he took AND the returned check fees, and apologizing to her. It was a very effective message, and my cousin did exactly that - pronto.

Men have a way of engaging with other men to get results. It is not to say that you cannot handle these situations. I am sure that once my mother recovered she would have dealt with my cousin accordingly. But if you could share the burden of resolving conflicts with someone who would be happy to do it because he cares for you, why would you not take advantage of that help? Allow your Leading Man to take care of you from time to time. I know you are strong, he knows you are strong, and you know you are strong; but you are also human, and you get tired. Allow your Leading Man to shoulder the burden while you rest. Share the load.

Leading Men are not intimidated by your success; they admire and respect it. They help you achieve more. CHROME men do what they can to help you when things get rough, and stand back to allow you to enjoy the pleasures when things go well. Leading Men inspire in you the desire to post the hash tag #ilovethatman. Understand though that the "love" here may be platonic. You just need it to be genuine so that he is worthy to be a member of your Crew.

So the tenth and final step to being the Leading Lady of YOUR life is to surround yourself with good, honorable men who care for you, are

there for you, and support your dreams as your own.

Everyday Men Who

Support the Leading Lady Legacy

Meet Charles "Chuck" Taylor. We have been friends since childhood and stay in contact, mostly through social media. I like to run (okay, I run to clear my mind and burn calories from too many cupcakes). One Saturday I did a 5K and posted the post-race picture to social media. I immediately regretted it. This 5K was my first race after my health crisis and I thought the picture would make me feel charged up and accomplished; instead, I felt defeated and tired because I did not like the way I looked. Before I could take it down, Chuck

132

commented on the picture with a congratulatory message: "I see you girl!" I felt worlds better because these four words refocused my mind on why I did the race and posted the picture in the first place: to celebrate my recovery and healing, not to model athletic wear.

Chuck is a son, brother, friend and longshoreman. He is a man of CHROME and understands the importance of being a supportive Leading Men, even when it is something small (or not so small) as posting encouraging words on social media.

The 10 Steps to Being the Leading Lady of YOUR Life ReCapped

1. Move through life to a tempo that makes YOU feel good

2. Take time to be peaceful and calm.

3. Maintain control over yourself.

4. Embrace your beauty and sense of style.

5. Love people to the best of your ability.

6. Accept that there will be missteps in life

7. Identify the members of your Crew.

8. Understand and communicate your wants and needs.

9. Like, love and believe in yourself.

10. Surround yourself with good, honorable men.

YOUR Leading Lady Legacy

"It's humbling and enthralling to know your legacy

when you're alive."

Laura Schlessinger

We talk about *legacy* throughout this book, but exactly what does it mean?   Legacy is defined as a gift or bequest; or anything handed down from the past, as from an ancestor or predecessor. **The Leading Lady Legacy is the gift that you give yourself and those who are influenced by you.** This is the fruit of your labor, to be enjoyed in your lifetime; and also what will be left behind for others to enjoy. Your legacy will become part of your legend, so it is important that whatever you decide to leave behind is worth sharing. You will know the wonder of the gift of your legacy when you feel joy when reflecting upon your actions and the positive results of your hard work, and watching others whom you inspired and influenced do marvelous things.

Throughout this book, I focus on everyday women because it is important that you know that you are influential and powerful no matter who you are, what job you hold, or where you live. If you interact with only one person every day, you can still be influential and have the opportunity to share your legacy of love with that one person. **If we all focused on making the three feet around us the best three feet in the world, how much better the world would be.**

Whenever you doubt your importance in the world, remember your strength and courage. Do not allow other people's brilliance make you feel dull and uninteresting. **You matter! You have purpose! You are a necessary part of this world!** We all have our parts to play in this drama of life. Take your role seriously and deliver your performance with gusto giving it all you have! And when you happen upon those rare moments of quiet time alone, congratulate yourself on your good work. Smile to yourself when you consider all you have overcome. Pat yourself on the back for being patient with the impatient, kind to the unkind, loving to the unloving, generous to the miserly, honest to the dishonest, fair to the unfair, and forgiving to the unmerciful. These are huge accomplishments that support and reinforce your legacy. They also make the world better because you are living as a shining example of how things should be, and how they could be if each of would only embrace our own legacy.

Your Leading Lady Affirmation

"You will be a failure, until you impress the subconscious with the conviction you are a success. This is done by making an affirmation which 'clicks." -

- Florence Scovel Shinn

My beautiful sister, you are THE Leading Lady of YOUR Life. The only person having the power to cede that position to someone else is you. Sometimes we do it unconsciously, yielding to other people's desires, positions, and stature because we think this is a way to convey respect. Other times we do it consciously as a way to keep the peace and minimize strife in our relationships. It is entirely possible and necessary that you maintain your ranking in your life as Number One AND convey to others that they are important and are held in high regard in your mind. It is a delicate balancing act, but one that you can and will do. I am claiming this for you. How? By affirming who you are, why you do what you do, and being clear about how you get things done. **This is your affirmation statement, your reason to be. This is your purpose, your passion, and your power!**

I created my first official affirmation statement January 2014 as part of my Launch Board movement (more on that later). I needed to understand what was important to me - personally, professionally, and spiritually - so that I could zero in on the things that were not in line with where I wanted to go in life. I thought it would be hard, but with the guidance of my life coach, it took less than an hour. That was one of the most valuable and useful slices of time that I have spent on myself in a long time. This is what I created:

"I am a powerful speaker, motivating others to be incomparable leaders, innovators, and lovers to empower themselves, their families, and their

communities. I am world renowned for my brilliant personality, thoughtful insight, and personable spirit. My success is derived from the love I feel for everyday people and my desire to make a positive, lasting impression on the world that resonates for generations to come."

This Power Statement is lofty, high minded, and ambitious. It stretches me to the very recesses of my mental and physical abilities, and ensures that I will not become complacent or bored with my incremental successes. I challenge you to take an hour for yourself to create an affirmation or Power Statement that does the same for you.

Step 1: Consider what excites you. What would you do absolutely free (or have done absolutely free) if you won the lottery today?

Step 2: Determine how you want people to feel when they leave your presence. Will they feel excited, inspired, happy, motivated, contented?

Step 3: Decide how you intend to accomplish Step 2. Through volunteerism or service, activism or advocacy, entrepreneurship, and/or a combination of all of the above?

Step 4: Analyze why you want to accomplish Step 2. Do you want fame, glory, acceptance, and/or love? Do you want to make the world a better place and leave it better than you found it? Do you want it all? Be honest with yourself. This is YOUR affirmation statement - you do not have to share it with anyone, and it is important that you understand what motivates you. Only then will you be able to shift gears (if necessary) or continue on the path you have chosen as it supports your goals and aspirations.

Step 5: Write your Power Statement being sure to make yourself the center point. "I am" is a great way to begin each sentence. This helps you stay focused on the central character here - YOU.

Step 6: Post your affirmation. My Power Statement is posted on my Launching Board. It is big, bold, and takes up a third of my poster. Because it is so prominently displayed, I see it at least once a day and am able to stay focused on my goals - it is a constant reminder of where I want to be and why.

Your affirmation or Power Statement will help keep you focused during the good times, and remind you how great you are during the rough patches. Take the time to commit to this statement as a gift to yourself. Consider it your leading lady's love gift!

The Leading Lady Legacy Launch Board

When you're getting ready to launch into space,

you're sitting on a big explosion waiting to happen.

Sally Ride

My Leading Lady sister, you have completed all the chapters of this book! I hope you are feeling energized and empowered, ready to put together a plan of action to make your dreams of living the Leading Lady Legacy a reality. This section of the book will guide you through the process of creating a Launch Board to make that happen. What is a Launch Board? You may have heard of a vision or action board. A launch board is a step beyond.

Wikihow.com defines a vision board as a "collage of images, pictures and affirmations of your dreams and all of the things that make you happy." And Dr. Neil Farber author of *The Blame Game* states that "vision boards are based on the Law of Attraction.

The idea that your mode of thinking directly affects what the universe gives you. If you put positive mental energy into the universe, you'll be the recipient of positive outcomes."

An action board is a vision board that also prompts you to envision the training or effort to get where you want to be, rather than the goal itself. Both action boarding and vision boarding have become big business. There are organizations that charge $595 per person to guide you through the creation of one. I am not asking for that. I am asking you to be open as I guide you through the process of creating a map that will help you to "write the vision and make it plain" and put it into action in the following pages. This is my way of living my legacy - sharing the knowledge I have with you, giving you more than what you expected in this book.

As stated before, vision and action boarding has become commercialized, but it is limiting because it typically encompasses only visual images. A launch board is different because it combines pictures and writing. It is based on the biblical concept of "Writing the vision and making it plain" found in the Old Testament book of Habakkuk. I know this book is not bible study, but there are two things that you need to know from Habakkuk to help you launch this next phase of your life as the Leading Lady: WRITE and WAIT.

Once we are aware of what we are charged to do in life, we must write it down. Writing commits us and shows the universe that we are serious. Writing is actually the easy part. The hard part is waiting. Why? Because we want to know what is going to happen and when it will happen to the moment - even if we are going to be late! How many times have you attended an event that was supposed to start at one time, you arrive after the start time, and they have not even started setting up yet? You may be happy that you did not miss anything, or frustrated that the program will run that much later. Either way, the program will begin, you will be a part of it, and if you frame your mind correctly, you may still enjoy it.

So how do we write our vision plain enough to create a road map for future success? Or better stated: what does it take to create a board that prepares you to launch? First, understand that your Launch Board is a guide that leads you through your aspirations by clearly defining what you want, creating a path to achieve those desires, and identifying the resources required to achieve success. Second, embrace the belief that this Launch Board is all about YOU. Everything that goes on this board must have you at the center. Next, set aside the items you will need to make a board worthy of your dreams: one large poster board, markers, magazines you love, a pen, table, comfortable chair, a quiet place, and two hours of dedicated time. Now you are ready to create your Launch Board.

Step 1: Close your eyes and take a moment to clear your mind. Take a series of deep breaths. Relax your body and just enjoy the silence.

Step 2: Ask the Creator to guide your hand. Do not ask for things, just listen.

Step 3: When you are ready to work, write what was revealed on the back of the poster board.

Step 4: Set realistic goals and time tables for those goals, and write them out on the back of the poster board, under your vision.

Now that you have created a plan of action, continue with the remaining steps.

Step 5: Browse the magazines you selected and cut out pictures that represent each goal.

Step 6: Paste the pictures on the board and beside each picture, write what it means to you and when you plan to achieve it. If you need help achieving a specific goal, (such as needed expertise or funding), then write that on the back of the board. Remember to phrase your statements in a positive manner. "I will achieve..." "This will happen...." You are the Leading Lady of YOUR life. You are powerful, and the source of the force to LAUNCH your board and your life! Also, do not feel compelled to fill the entire board – when you are done, you are done.

Step 7: Post your board in a place where you may reference it on a regular basis so you may keep on track and remember why you are doing the things you are doing. But do not dwell on the board, and if changes need to be made to the timeline or the actions to get things done, be flexible. Rome was not built in a day, and neither will the culmination of your dreams.

Now comes the waiting. How do you know when it is time to move on the actions recorded on your board? When is the best time to launch? I have a secret. I can tell you the exact moment your time to move or launch came: the minute you picked up this book. I know that because you came to this book, to this passage, when you were ready to read and receive it. Your time is now because you are here. You were watching and waiting for the "sign." You saw this book and purchased it because you were ready to do a new thing in your life.

The time to move is NOW. The time to launch is upon you. The only thing holding you back is YOU. Commit to removing yourself as an obstacle to your success and get ready, set, and LAUNCH!

Conclusion

My dear sister, we made it! You now have the 10 steps to become the Leading Lady of Your life. It is my sincere hope that the information set forth in this book helps you to embrace the beauty that is you and you alone. I am excited about the transformations that are in progress and look forward to seeing the end results. Let us connect on social media and exchange Leading Lady Legacy strides. My Twitter handle is @lynitamb and I am on Facebook as Lynita Mitchell-Blackwell and Leading Through Living Community. I wish the best in everything you do and cannot wait to see all the Leading Ladies emerge!

THE BEGINNING

Thank you for taking time to read ***The Leading Lady Legacy: 10 Steps to Becoming the Leading Lady of YOUR Life!*** If you enjoyed it, please consider telling your friends or posting a short review. Word of mouth is an author's best friend and much

appreciated.

About the Author

Lynita Mitchell-Blackwell is a **LEADERSHIP CHAMPION**! Leveraging several years in Corporate America as a **CPA**, managing **attorney** of her law firm, **executive recruiter** of C-suite professionals, and **leader** of several professional and social organizations, Lynita now utilizes the experience gained in those empowering roles to encourage, equip, and **CHAMPION** people to be leaders professionally, personally, and within their communities.

Photo by "Picture Lady Pinkie" Webster

As the Chief Leadership Officer of the **Leading Through Living Community**, Lynita designs, leads, and executes workshops, seminars, and motivational speeches that position professionals and emerging executives for success!

Areas of specialization include:

• Strategic Personal and Business Image and Brand Management
• Effective Digital Platform Engagement
• Successful Career Transitions
• Fast - and Legal! - Business Development Methodologies
• Team Building, Management, & Empowerment Techniques

Lynita is the author of two books: *The Leading Lady Legacy: 10 Steps to Becoming the Leading Lady of YOUR Life* and *Leading Through Living: A Guide for Women Seeking Growth Through Leadership*; and is founder and Editor-in-Chief of *BOLD Favor Magazine* that highlights BOLD people, organizations and causes that inspire us to live fearlessly in the areas of Leadership, Human Dignity, Spirituality, Empowered Style, Meaningful Relationships, and Health & Wellness.

Lynita has been honored to serve as a delegate to the 2014 Art of Living Foundation International Women's Conference in Bangalore, India; receive the 2012 President's Call to Service Award presented by the US President's Council on Service and Civic Participation; and recognized as a 2011 *Black Enterprise Magazine* Young & Bold Business Leader.

Lynita is a member of the board of directors of the LiT College Tour, the Executive Committee of the Douglas County Democratic Party, and Women in the Spotlight Goinglobal. She is a past president of the Georgia Chapter of the American Association of Attorney-CPA's, the Georgia Association of Black Women Attorneys Foundation, and a past Chair of the Advisory Board of the New Leaders Council - Atlanta Chapter.

Lynita is married to Rev. Brian K. Blackwell; they are the proud parents of one daughter.

www.ingramcontent.com/pod-product-compliance
Lightning Source LLC
Chambersburg PA
CBHW052011090426
42741CB00008B/1643